AWAKENINGS

J. TERRY JOHNSON

AWAKENINGS

DEFINING MOMENTS
IN A YOUNG MAN'S LIFE

Awakenings, Defining Moments in a Young Man's Life
Copyright © 2010 by J. Terry Johnson. All rights reserved.

This novel is a work of nonfiction. Names, descriptions, entities, and incidents included in the story are based on the lives of real people.

The opinions expressed by the author are not necessarily those of Tate Publishing, LLC.

Published by Tate Publishing & Enterprises, LLC
127 E. Trade Center Terrace | Mustang, Oklahoma 73064 USA
1.888.361.9473 | www.tatepublishing.com

Tate Publishing is committed to excellence in the publishing industry. The company reflects the philosophy established by the founders, based on Psalm 68:11,
"The Lord gave the word and great was the company of those who published it."

Book design copyright © 2010 by Tate Publishing, LLC. All rights reserved.
Cover design by Amber Gulilat
Interior design by Jeff Fisher
Editing by Emily Wilson

Published in the United States of America

ISBN: 978-1-61663-482-7
1. Biography & Autobiography, Personal Memoirs
2. Biography & Autobiography, Religious
10.08.06

DEDICATION

This book is dedicated to the memory of Jerry Wheeler, Janice Novak, Karen Hetrick, Sharon Stewart, Jacqulin Watson, and Angie Watson whose lives were cut short by unwelcomed tragedy, but whose influence for good extends far beyond their six windswept graves.

ACKNOWLEDGMENTS

Higher education is one of America's greatest treasures. Each year students from all over the world seek admission to American colleges and universities because these institutions have established a reputation for being among the premier learning centers on the planet. It was my privilege to graduate from two of our nation's finest, Oklahoma Christian College and Southern Methodist University.

I will always be indebted to those who taught my college courses and others who performed vital roles of administrative service. They helped me work through the *defining moments* in my own life and supported the critical decisions that I made while maturing from adolescence to young adulthood. Those life choices have blessed me time and again as I have pursued my own career and even now as I reinvent myself in retirement.

Awakenings is my final offering in a trilogy of novellas (*Cardinal Fever,* 2009 and *Kirby: from the Baseball Field to the Battlefield,* 2008), all published by Tate Publishing. The staff continues to provide me with outstanding professional support. My special thanks are extended to Emily Wilson for her editing skills and to Amber Gulilat for her cover design and to Jeff Fisher for his layout concepts. Terry Cordingley has led the marketing strategies for all three publications, and Chris Castor has designed the web page—*jtj.tatepublishing. net*—where all of the books are currently showcased.

I find it impossible to convey the full measure of my appreciation for Pat Boone's willingness to write the foreword to *Awakenings.* He was at the top of the music charts when most of these events occurred. His book, *Twixt Twelve and Twenty,* was a refreshing point of view for many of us who grew up in the late 1950s and early 1960s. Pat is an excellent example of a young man who had to make some career-shaping decisions early in his life and has lived long enough to see the blessings that come to those who choose to do what is *right* rather than what is *popular*. His brother Nick Boone and nephew Grant Boone also deserve my thanks for their counsel and assistance.

CONTENTS

FOREWORD

Although I've always enjoyed living in the present, there are occasions when I relish the opportunity to steal a glance over my shoulder and recall events that took place years ago. I have great memories of growing up in Nashville, my freshman year at David Lipscomb College, dating Shirley, and the whirlwind career that pulled me up by my roots and planted me in the entertainment business. Some of the details have been blurred by the passing of time, but the major themes are as fresh as if they had occurred yesterday.

That's why I've enjoyed reading *Awakenings: Defining Moments in a Young Man's Life* and recommend it to you. The book's author, J. Terry Johnson, invites the reader to revisit the burning questions that beg for answers during our late adolescence and early adulthood. *Who am I? What is my destiny? Is there a lifetime companion in my future? If so, who might that be?* As I reflect on those questions, they remind me of the themes I developed forty-plus years ago in my own book, *Twixt Twelve and Twenty*.

Awakenings is an accurate portrayal of the many common uncertainties that kept us in a fog as we passed through adolescence and became responsible young adults. Our slate was clean, and we preferred that it remain that way; yet there were so many chances for misstepping as we made our fundamental life choices. Making those decisions in a supportive, Christian environment—for Terry and me—made all the difference in the world.

I have always been a fan of Christian education. In Nashville, I attended David Lipscomb high school and college, and in recent years, I've served as Chairman of the Advisory Board of Pepperdine University. From what I've observed, young people address the major decisions in their lives with greater confidence and with more support when they are taught by spiritually minded professors on a Christian college campus. After reading *Awakenings,* I am even more convinced this premise is true.

In 1961, Terry Johnson and I were ships passing in the night. Two days before Terry enrolled as a sophomore at Oklahoma Christian College, I participated in a Labor Day rally on the OCC campus to raise financial support for the college. The film crew for my new movie, *State Fair,* was shooting a few scenes on the racetrack at the Oklahoma City Fairgrounds. In addition to the rally, I recall spending time with the OCC students at their evening devotional. Had Terry arrived on campus two days earlier, we might have met. I wish we had, but now we have—in his book!

Set aside an hour or two to read *Awakenings.* I'm confident you will enjoy the reflective narrative of a young man as he confronts the major issues in his life. Share it with your children or grandchildren who have those decisions ahead of them. It will produce a blessing. After all, most of us learn more from example than precept. *Awakenings* is both.

—Pat Boone

Pat Boone speaking to college students at
Oklahoma Christian College - 1961

PHIKEIAS

Whoever came up with the name "hell week" nailed it. The past four days had been unlike anything I could have imagined when I decided to pledge a Greek fraternity. My favorite uncle, who had been a Phi Delt thirty-five years ago at Westminster College in Fulton, Missouri, encouraged me to consider a fraternity in order to get better acquainted with other members of the freshman class. That made sense, so I accepted a bid from the Phi Delta Theta chapter at Southern Methodist University and joined its pledge class, the Phikeias (FĪ KĪ′ YĂHS).

Harassment and humiliation began almost immediately. We uninitiated pledges spent five torturous months proving ourselves worthy to be considered for "active status." It was an endurance test, and as might be expected, there were casualties along the way.

Most of the hazing was moderately administered. We were required to serenade the coeds on sorority row, shine shoes for the brothers, serve meals at the frat house, and run a host of errands as directed by the upperclassmen.

Occasionally, one of the Phikeias would be singled out for having shown disrespect. After being verbally berated by the brothers, the lowly pledge would be stripped to his underwear and put through a strenuous round of calisthenics. The whole process was designed to test the mettle of us younger men and see if we were capable of being submissive to authority.

Now, here I was, lying flat on my stomach in the middle of some field north of Dallas, being driven to physical exertion beyond my own limits—all to prove that I was *worthy.*

"What do you think you're doing, Phikeia?" a smart-mouthed sophomore yelled into my ear. "Did I say you could take a break? Give me ten more, and don't let me see your stomach hit the ground until I say so!"

"Yes, sir," I replied, barely able to speak.

"What did you say?" the self-appointed drill sergeant retorted.

"Yes sir!" I thundered and began working on ten more push-ups. Every muscle in both arms quivered as I counted them out. "One, two, three, four…"

The sky was as black as a tar pit, clouds hiding even the slightest glimmer of celestial light. The north wind had become stronger in the last hour, and I felt mist in the air. In the distance, I could see faint lights from the city twinkling on the horizon, and from every side, I heard jibes and taunts directed to other members of my pledge class.

"Harris, on your feet!" another cocky sophomore screamed at the fatigued Phikeia to my left.

Jim Harris was the son of a physician from Marshall, Texas. He and I had become good friends during the year, double-dating a few times and hanging out at the movie theaters on weekends. Now we were starring in our own horror flick, staggering to the climax of a ghoulish script.

"I said *run* in place, Phikeia, not mosey!" Jim's tormenter bellowed. "Lift up those knees, and get that smirk off your face."

It was past midnight, and I was physically and emotionally spent. For the last four hours, the freshmen had been called upon to "rally" as one of the final steps before being accepted as true "brothers in the bond." We had been warned that tonight would be the *mother of all rallies,* but I had not been prepared for the physical toll being taken on my weary body. Another hour of this punishment and they could ship me home in a box.

Mercifully, Gus Comiskey, a senior who had adopted me as his little brother, knelt down near my head and said, "Just hang on for a few minutes. I think the worst is over."

I hadn't come this far to give up. If Gus thought the worst was over, I believed him. *Just hang on,* I mentally repeated to myself and waited for my next directive.

Gus Comiskey

Within a few minutes, the pledge class was herded into automobiles and transported back to campus. I was trying not to make eye contact with anyone, and others were doing the same. The less attention we called to ourselves, the less verbal abuse we incurred from the brothers.

As the caravan approached fraternity row on the east side of the campus, our driver instructed the Phikeias to line up at the rear door of the Phi Delt house in single-file. "Once you get to the door, you'll learn what to do next," he continued. And then we piled out of his smelly coupe and did as we had been told.

There we were, a disheveled crew, beaten down by the events of the past few days, but anxious to experience whatever lay ahead. These insufferable sophomores, who had excelled as whip-crackers at the rally, had survived similar treatment the year before. That thought alone was consoling and gave us freshmen new resolve to stay the course.

Bud Nichols, a popular football star and one of the more pleasant upperclassmen among the brothers, stood at the door with bandanas in his hand. "Tie these around your head, covering your eyes," he said as he handed one to each pledge. "Someone will lead you from here to your next rally stop."

I watched as my pledge brothers began folding the red and black cloths, fitting them snugly over their eyes and tying them behind their heads. What a group of guys—Jim Harris, Charlie Younger, John Buck, Bob McCain, and others just like them—all young men with promising futures. They appeared to thrive in this environment, whereas I always felt a bit out of my league.

Was it their wealth or perhaps their more liberated lifestyle? Or was it just my imagination making a racket between my ears? Most of my pledge brothers had their own cars and plenty of spending cash. They were at ease attending the keg parties and seemingly comfortable dating the society girls on sorority row. I liked these guys. I really did! But, I had an anxious feeling that I was miscast in their script.

My high school counselors had told me that the college years would bring me to a new state of self-awareness. There would be answers to the questions: *Who am I? What career path is right for me? And who am I looking for to be my wife, someone to be my lifelong partner and the mother of my children?* If those were the questions, I had already spent the better part of my freshman year at the university and didn't have a clue what the answers should be.

No time to think about that now. Blindfolds securely in place, we were led upstairs and into a room that had been off-limits to Phikeias—until now. Although we sensed that others were present, the quietness was deafening. Finally, the door was shut and we were instructed to remove our blindfolds.

My first impression of the chapter room was *ho-*

hum. Perhaps I had been expecting too much, like gold-gilded furnishings and marble-covered walls. It was nothing like that.

A small table, with four wooden chairs facing the rear door, sat at the front of the room. National, state, and fraternal flags decorated the front wall. Straight-backed, armless chairs, lining both sides of the room, were positioned facing the opposite wall. The brothers were seated in those chairs while the pledge class sat as a huddled mass in the center of the hardwood floor.

Jack Knox, a senior from Grand Saline, Texas, and president of the chapter, sat at the table with his fellow officers. After a few opening remarks from the sergeant-at-arms, the Phikeia class was presented to the brothers as having completed its pledge requirements and was now recommended for active membership in the fraternity.

"Welcome to our chapter room," Knox began. "You have demonstrated courage and persistence in your journey to become a member of this fraternity. I want to be the first to welcome you as an active brother in the Texas Delta Chapter of Phi Delta Theta."

Those were the words I had wanted to hear, and I relished the moment, receiving congratulations from

Phikeias and upperclassmen alike. It would take a few days for the achievement of the past few months to sink in—and for my sore muscles to recover. But for now, I took personal satisfaction in having survived. I had become a "brother in the bond."

A RUN
FOR THE BORDER

From an early age, I had fallen in love with Dallas. My mom and I had made numerous trips to visit my Aunt Daisy and Uncle Charles Steineger, who lived near University Park in Dallas, or as we referred to it, "Big D." Twice while I was in elementary school, my dad had taken me to the train depot in Springfield, Missouri, placed me on the *Texas Special*, tipped the porter $10 to look after me, and sent me all alone on the ten-hour trip to Dallas.

Everything was super-sized in Big D. The downtown buildings stretched far into the sky and were bejeweled at night with an overcoat of glorious lights. The Magnolia Building, adorned with an illuminated red Pegasus, was my personal favorite. It could be seen from just about anywhere in the downtown area and was one of the city's most recognizable landmarks.

There was even a smell about Dallas that I liked. It had something to do with a sticky layer of black clay that lay beneath the city lawns and gardens, stretching into the farmlands that began only a few miles outside the city limits. Even with both eyes shut, I could tell if I were anywhere near Dallas in the summer months.

Aunt Daisy was an avid gardener, having won many blue ribbons for her stunning floral arrangements. She had authored books, illustrated with her innovative floral bouquets, and had spoken throughout the state on flower gardening. In the early evenings, Uncle Charles and I would help her water the beds and pick some of the blooms she would use for an upcoming lecture.

Spending summers with my aunt and uncle contributed enormously to my growing love affair with Dallas. A year before she died of Hodgkin's disease, Aunt Daisy took me on a tour of Southern Methodist University. I was twelve years old and about to begin junior high school.

"I want you to meet a friend of mine," she said as I hopped into the passenger seat of her blue and white Chevy convertible. "Your mother went to SMU, and you may want to do the same when you're ready for college."

The university campus on Mockingbird Lane was impressive. Stately live oak trees lined the narrow streets, and large fountains graced the central mall. The buildings, all constructed with red bricks, were beautifully designed in classical Georgian-styled architecture.

Parking her car in a lot near the main quadrangle, Aunt Daisy led me to the steps of Dallas Hall, famous for its handsome dome, covering an equally impressive rotunda. A portly man, dressed in a frumpy tweed sports jacket and carrying a black briefcase, directed her to the offices of her friend, Dean Mayne Longnecker.

"Well, who do we have here?" Dean Longnecker asked as he emerged from his office.

"I want you to meet my nephew from Missouri," Aunt Daisy answered. "You remember my sister, Jeanne?"

Dallas Hall - SMU

"Yes, of course," he replied.

"Well, this is her eldest son, and I thought he might want to attend your university in a few years," she said with a broad smile.

We chatted a few minutes at the dean's offices and then went on a brief tour to the student union where summer school students were enjoying a break between classes. In less than an hour, a seed had been sown that grew over a few years into a ravenous urge to attend SMU. Six years would pass before I had to make that choice, but throughout junior and senior high school, I gave no other college or university serious consideration. I stubbornly held on to my dream of becoming a Mustang at SMU.

My dream, now a reality, was playing itself out in a suitable fashion, but there were a few black holes that wouldn't go away. Although classes were challenging, they were well within my academic comfort zone. First semester grades had been slightly above a B average.

Choosing a major was proving more difficult. I had always considered English my best subject, but every week my English professor's red pen had a field day making ugly notations all over my latest attempt to write a cogent essay. On at least two occasions, my essay had been returned with an enormous "F" written at the top of the first page. I was humiliated and frightened. Eventually, I began to contemplate other disciplines for my major field of study, and that led me to examine a host of alternative career choices.

Baseball, which had been such a big part of my life during high school, was still important in college. I had tried out for the freshman team, the SMU Ponies, and made the squad as a second-baseman. We were just getting into the spring season, but I could already tell that playing for a freshman team in the Southwest Conference was not going to be as much fun as the American Legion Junior Baseball program had been the past three summers in Missouri. Had I outgrown the game, or should I pursue it with renewed vigor? Another black hole!

Then there was the dating scene. With no car and very little spending cash, prospects were not too promising. My Phikeia brothers were thoughtful to set me up with their girlfriends' sorority sisters and offered to double date using their cars, but I felt more like a prop in someone else's play. Old flames in Springfield had burnt out, and I didn't see any new sparks developing with the girls I had met in Dallas.

"You're just the guy I've been looking for," said Jim Harris as we bumped into each other in the parking lot of the Phi Delt house. Jim was always stirring up something and kept my life interesting. "You've been drafted; go with us to Nuevo Laredo this weekend. We need a 'designated driver.'"

"Nuevo Laredo? Where's that?" I said, trying to determine if this was for real or just a prank.

"Mexico, man! We're going to Mexico! It's spring break," Jim said jubilantly. "You'll be the only one sober. The rest of us plan to get drunker than skunks. Meet us here at the Phi house after classes on Thursday. You're driving my car."

Had I given the matter a second thought, I likely would have declined his proposition. But, it was spring break and I had never been to Mexico. Jim made it sound as if the guys really needed me, so no big deal. I agreed to be their driver.

Awakenings

On a map, it looked so easy. Here was Dallas, and there was Laredo, a Texas border town across the Rio Grande from Mexico. Both cities were in the same state. What I had not calculated was the massive expanse of Texas. Border to border was a long haul. Talking a friendly Texas Ranger out of a speeding ticket somewhere south of San Antonio made the trip at least twenty minutes longer. When we pulled into Laredo just before midnight, I was the only one in the car who was both awake and sober.

Crossing the border proved uneventful. The guards on either side of the Rio Grande had seen it all. They knew a car full of college-age boys might get into a little mischief, but they were no threat to anyone but themselves. So, they allowed us entry into Mexico—the first time I had ever set foot outside the United States.

Finding a motel room for five guys in Nuevo Laredo after midnight was not quite so easy. What we settled on was not much better than a one-room tenement in any Shantytown, USA. The place reeked of cigar smoke and liquor, and there was only one bed. We threw the mattress on the floor. Two slept on it, two others on the box springs, and I made a pallet in the corner of the room on the filthy tiled floor.

None of us awoke early, but when we finally began to stir, it didn't take us long to greet the day. Spending any part of the daytime in our motel room was not very appealing. Besides, we were hungry.

If there was an attractive neighborhood in Nuevo Laredo, I never found it. I should have known that my colleagues were not on a sight-seeing trip. They began barhopping before noon and didn't stop until the wee hours of the next morning.

I wiled the time away souvenir shopping in the local plaza, hanging out in the lobby of a small hotel, and reading a paperback novel I had brought from campus. Every few hours, I would check on the guys as they flitted in and out of foul-smelling bars and bordellos. What they did there was their business, but I was worried someone might lock horns with the wrong person and get hurt.

The closest we came to an incident was when one of our *compadres,* drunk almost to the point of unconsciousness, was thrown out of a bar and left face down in a dusty street. It was time to go home—and we did.

That weekend trip to Mexico left me with an unsettled feeling in the pit of my stomach. I hadn't broken any of my self-imposed rules of personal behavior. No alcohol was consumed by me, and I made no play for any of the barroom senoritas. But it had all been within my grasp. Temptation had knocked at the door. Was I living closer to the edge than I really cared to admit?

As much as I loved being in Dallas and as highly as I regarded the education I was receiving at SMU, this was not where I wanted to spend the next three years of my life. Yet, if not here, then where? I had no answers to a very perplexing puzzle.

THE MAN
FROM OKLAHOMA

The spring semester was rapidly coming to a close. In three weeks, I would take my final exams and return to Missouri for the summer. Grades were decent, but not quite as robust as they had been in the fall. The combination of enduring "hell week" and missing too many classes for baseball games had taken a small toll on my GPA.

Throughout the year, I had made church attendance on Sunday mornings a priority. Rarely did I try to attend Sunday or Wednesday night services, but on Sunday morning, I could usually be found attending Dr. John

Bell's Bible class, followed by the inspirational worship assembly at the Skillman Avenue Church of Christ.

When it came to church attendance, not having a car was definitely a handicap. Fifty freshman boys resided on the second floor of the west wing of Boaz Hall. Three or four of those residents made it their practice to attend Sunday morning services every week—most of them walking to the Methodist church on the southwest corner of the campus.

Fortunately, I had met Bill Banister, a graduate student whose father, John Banister, preached for the Skillman Avenue church. Bill was faithful to swing by Boaz Hall each Sunday morning or arrange for someone else to provide me with a ride to services. I hated being such a nuisance but could think of no viable alternative.

"How's your week gone?" Bill asked as we made our way through the light Sunday morning traffic.

"Not bad," I answered, suppressing a tale-tell yawn that suggested the week had been long and sleep had been scarce.

"You're in for a treat today," he said, glancing at his watch. "Dad is away this week on another speaking engagement. A man from Oklahoma is going to be our guest preacher." He may have mentioned the man's name, but it never registered.

More than a thousand Christians worshipped at Skillman Avenue each Sunday morning. The spacious auditorium was tastefully decorated with tall windows; deep red-wine carpet, cushioned pews, and white wood trim in abundance, making every color in the building seem even brighter. The design magazines would have described the decor as "Southern elegance."

I had not made any close friends at church and usually sat alone. Bill, engaged to be married, usually sat with his fiancée, JoAnn. They often sat with young professionals who were older than I. If there were other students from SMU in attendance, I had not met them.

A typical service included congregational singing, prayers, Scripture readings, observing the Lord's Supper, and listening to a Bible-centered sermon from Bill's father. The only variation on this Sunday's program was that one of the elders was slated to introduce the man from Oklahoma as our preacher for the day.

"We are privileged to have Dr. James O. Baird as our guest speaker," intoned the stoop-shouldered bishop. "He is the president of Oklahoma Christian College in Oklahoma City."

My head jerked, and I sat up straight in my seat. I knew this man! He had visited with my parents and me in Missouri a year ago and had tried to persuade me to attend his college instead of SMU. *Yes,* I recognized him now. What a coincidence!

I was especially attentive to the sermon that morning. Dr. Baird, balding pre-maturely and wearing thick eyeglasses, stood tall and erect in the pulpit. He had a winsome smile and a genteel manner that likely came from his Tennessee roots.

An articulate speaker, Dr. Baird presented a powerful lesson on the resurrection of Jesus Christ. His approach to the subject was fresh and compelling. On the back of an attendance card, I took a few notes, outlining the sermon and scribbling down his biblical references.

After the closing prayer, I made my way to the foyer, hoping to find Dr. Baird. A crowd of well-wishers had gathered around him to extend greetings, and I waited patiently until it was my turn to do the same.

James O. Baird

"Dr. Baird, you may not remember, but last May you visited with my parents and me while you were in Springfield, Missouri," I said.

"As a matter of fact, I do remember you," he said warmly. "How's your year going at SMU?"

"Oh, all right," I replied, not wanting to reveal my personal quandary as to whether I would return in the fall.

Then he surprised me when he asked, "Have you ever given any thought of becoming a preacher?"

"As a matter of fact, I have," I confided. "I've also been considering law with an undergraduate degree in English."

"Let me get your address," Dr. Baird said, reaching for a pen inside his coat pocket. "I want to send you a packet of materials from Oklahoma Christian. If you would entertain the thought of transferring next fall, I might be able to find some scholarship assistance."

"Thank you," I responded. "I'd be glad to hear from you."

I gave him my post office box number at the SMU student union. He jotted it on a business card, writing almost upside down with his left hand. We parted, saying our good-byes, and I wondered whether our paths would ever cross again.

On Wednesday, I pulled an envelope out of my post office box and read the return address:

Office of the President
Oklahoma Christian College
Route 1, Box 141
Oklahoma City, OK 73111

I tore the envelope open and grasped the letter that was folded inside. There it was, in the second paragraph, the offer I had hoped to receive: "a transfer scholarship in the amount of $100 will be credited to your account, $50 for the fall term and $50 for the spring…"

Well, that wasn't exactly the amount of financial assistance I had hoped to receive, but it was an offer and it was from the president himself. The only way I would ever know whether I might be suited for ministry would be to take a crack at some legitimate courses in biblical studies. I began to see a little daylight around some of my black holes.

On the last day of finals, I ran into Jim Harris as we were both coming out of a biology exam.

"It's been fun," Jim said. "See you next fall?"

"I don't think so, Jim," I replied, hating to break the news. "I plan to transfer next fall to Oklahoma Christian College in Oklahoma City."

"What's the deal?" Jim asked. He couldn't believe what he had heard.

"I'm not sure, but I've been giving some thought to studying for the ministry," I managed to say, not knowing whether Jim would take me seriously or laugh in my face. "It's one of two options I've been toying with, and I won't know my own heart unless I give it a try."

"Do they have a Phi Delt chapter there?" Jim inquired.

"As far as I can tell, they don't have fraternities or sororities of any kind," I answered.

Jim was not impressed but was gracious and wished me well. We promised to keep in touch during the summer. I sensed that a chapter in my life was closing and wondered whether the new chapter would be for better or for worse. Time would tell.

MANAGING
DISAPPOINTMENT

Had I taken the time to visit Oklahoma Christian College before showing up for my sophomore year, I might not have enrolled at all. The differences between SMU and OCC were enormous.

For starters, I had left my beloved Dallas for a wide spot on the prairie where the wind blew incessantly. SMU was a five-thousand-student university with a solid academic reputation and played NCAA intercollegiate athletics in the prestigious Southwest Conference; OCC was a 375-student college, unaffiliated in its fledgling athletic program, and had neither graduated its first senior class nor secured its accreditation as a four-year college with the North Central Association. What was I thinking?

The campus in Oklahoma City was nothing like the picture postcard I had left on Mockingbird Lane. At best, the Oklahoma campus could be described as *stark*. Five years earlier the site had been nothing more than two hundred acres of red clay, with sporadic outcroppings of native prairie grass and long stretches of barbed-wire fence. There were no live oak trees spreading huge limbs tip to tip. Instead, scores of little saplings, small enough that I could pet their tops, dotted the landscape and a few scruffy-looking oak trees, clustered in a wide drainage area, had grown to a height of twenty feet.

At least the buildings at Oklahoma Christian were relatively new and well maintained. They were small, one- and two-story, rectangular-shaped modules with flat, commercial-styled roofs. All were constructed with red brick and a white fascia band trimming the roofline, providing an attractive, unified appearance.

OCC campus in early 1960s

Having no central corridors, all residence hall rooms opened to the outside. If you didn't know you were looking at a campus, you might confuse it for a tourist court. Sidewalks and paved parking lots, to connect the residence halls with the lone academic quadrangle, were virtually non-existent.

What I found that did please me were the students and the faculty. My roommate, Don Young, was a returning sophomore math major from Mangum, Oklahoma. Each morning he set a five o'clock alarm and made dreadful smelling instant coffee while listening to pop music on WKY-930 AM radio. Thirty minutes later, he quietly closed the outside door and left for his job at a local dairy farm where he milked a barnful of cows. Don knew all of the returning upperclassmen and helped me get acquainted with a few of his friends.

"This is Jerry Wheeler," Don said one afternoon as I happened to meet him and Jerry at the student mailboxes.

"You're in my Church History class," I said, recognizing the slim, bespeckled young scholar. "Where are you from?"

"Wichita, Kansas," Jerry replied.

"Are there very many students here from Kansas?" I asked quizzically.

Jerry smiled. "Oh, we have a pretty good Jayhawk contingent, all right. You'll be surprised." Then Jerry changed the subject. "What's with your letter sweater? Is that from high school?"

"No, I played freshman baseball last year at SMU," I answered with some embarrassment. It had never dawned on me that someone might confuse my only "trophy" from SMU with a common letter jacket from high school.

A few weeks later, I received a note to drop by President Baird's office. Since arriving on campus, I had seen Dr. Baird from a distance but had not tried to meet with him. Now I was being summoned to his corner office in the administration building.

"Come in. Have a seat," Dr. Baird said as he gestured toward a small, contemporary-styled couch that was crammed into his cozy, but crowded, office. "How's the year going for you?"

Same question as last spring, I thought, *but this time in an entirely different setting.*

"Classes are fine," I assured him, "but the campus is a little remote. I'm finding it difficult to go anywhere without a car."

We chatted several minutes about my classes and professors, and then he gave me some unsolicited advice.

"I've heard that you're doing well in your classes, but let me offer this caution: college is much more than books and lectures," he said pleasantly, yet with enough firmness to get my undivided attention. "You may need to reach out more socially—meet more students, join one of the social-service clubs, attend more of the extra-curricular events. Oh, and one more little thing. You may be sending a signal of mixed loyalty or social elitism by wearing your SMU letter sweater. Just a thought for what it's worth."

I pondered Dr. Baird's advice for several days before acting upon it. He was probably right about my being single-focused on academics. For the first two months, I had immersed myself in my studies and had been rewarded with a 4.0 GPA at midterm. What I lacked was the balance that makes a person successful with people in social settings. I was developing a reputation for being a snob.

Before the semester concluded, I had joined the Dorians, a social-service club with open membership for men and women. Students at Oklahoma Christian chose to be members of the Trojans, Bereans, Athenians, Spartans, Olympians, or Dorians rather than pledging a traditional Greek fraternity or sorority. All of the social-service clubs were designed to help students develop close friends, and most were open to students of both genders.

These student organizations were light-years from Phi Delta Theta, but the Dorians provided me with a core group of friends to hang out with, participate in intramurals, and go off campus for some group outings. I left my SMU letter sweater in my closet and launched a new course of social behavior.

A daily chapel service, required of all students, was held at ten a.m. in Cogswell-Alexander Auditorium. Male students and faculty or staff members led a devotional each morning, Monday through Friday, and a host of announcements were shared with the entire campus community. Students sat in assigned seats, and attendance was monitored by fellow classmates we called "chapel checkers."

One morning, immediately following chapel, I overheard a conversation between Jerry Wheeler and Guy Ross, another popular sophomore from Holdenville, Oklahoma.

"That's what I've heard," Jerry said in a quiet, solemn voice. "They've already kicked them out."

"For drinking or for being drunk?" Guy said, pressing Jerry for more details.

"Drinking," Jerry replied, "or maybe for just having some beer cans in their possession."

I was incredulous. Three of our classmates had been dismissed from school for drinking some beer. That sounded like a very harsh punishment to me. Drinking beer was not something I ever wanted to do, and it had never been a serious temptation for me; but, the idea that students had been dismissed from college because they had drunk a beer or two blew me away.

That afternoon, I made an appointment to see Dr. Joseph F. Jones, Dean of Students and the professor who taught my Church History class.

"I'm not at liberty to divulge any more details," Dean Jones explained. "We have rules, and these young men knew what the consequences would be for their actions."

Dean Jones and I debated the dismissal amicably for several minutes before I said, "Dr. Jones, it appears to me that the administration wanted to make an example of these three students. That isn't fair."

His response was stern and forthcoming. "You have every right to question whether the college should have a rule that calls for automatic expulsion of students who violate our drinking rules, but you have no right to question the motives of those who must administer those rules. Do you understand the difference?"

Right between the eyes! "Yes sir," I said as I rose to my feet and made a hasty exit.

Oklahoma Christian College was a decent place to obtain an education, but it wasn't the garden of Eden. I was finishing the term with mixed emotions. Should

I continue my education here or return to SMU, or possibly go back home and try one of the universities in Missouri? I needed to make some decisions during the Christmas break. Final exams were scheduled for mid-January, and after they were completed, the spring semester would begin.

THE TURNING POINT

etermined to remain at Oklahoma Christian for one more semester, I returned from Christmas holidays and prepared for final exams. I was carrying an eighteen-hour load, taking two courses in Bible, two in history, and one each from the English and science departments. Most of the professors had promised comprehensive examinations covering material presented throughout the entire semester.

After spending long hours in the library, cramming for six exams, I survived the ordeal and found my name listed on the Dean's Honor Roll. It was sweet victory for having made academics my primary focus over the past four and a half months. The last exam was hardly over before we lined up for registration and began the chase once again.

Without a car, it was almost impossible to hold an off-campus job, and on-campus jobs paid fifty cents per hour. Some students worked in the cafeteria while others served as janitors, cleaning one or more of the buildings. I had no aversion to working, but none of those positions appealed to me.

One day I checked my mailbox and found a memo asking that I make an appointment to visit with President Baird.

"Come in," the president said, welcoming me to his office. "Congratulations on making the Dean's List. Can you do it again this semester?"

"I'm going to try," I offered the obligatory reply. "But I plan to play baseball this spring. That may take some time away from my studies."

"Good for you," Dr. Baird flashed that warm, reassuring smile. "You need some balance in your life, and we need some good athletes on the baseball field."

"Listen, I have another proposition to throw at you," Dr. Baird said with a more somber tone in his voice. "How would you like a part-time job as a student recruiter? The college will pay you one dollar per hour for your time and make one of our pool cars available for you to use when you make off-campus appointments."

Needing some extra spending cash, I swung on the first pitch. "Yes!" I said before giving the matter a second thought.

"Good. You will need to meet with Phil Watson, our Vice President for Development," Dr. Baird continued. "He'll be able to explain more of what we would like for you to do in this role."

I jotted Mr. Watson's name down in my spiral notebook, stood up, and extended my hand to the president. "Thank you," I said. "I can use the money, and the job sounds like a lot of fun."

"Oh, and by the way," Dr. Baird said with a twinkle in his eye, "I would like for you and Julie Smith to come by my office tomorrow after chapel. The college has an opportunity to submit a color photograph for the cover of *Teenage Christian* magazine, and I want the two of you to be in it."

I left President Baird's office with a better feeling about the new semester. Baseball, a job that paid a dollar an hour, an occasional opportunity to have some wheels, and a photo shoot with Julie Smith, the most attractive girl in the sophomore class; things were looking up.

Teenage Christian Magazine - 1962

Intercollegiate baseball at Oklahoma Christian was a farce. There were no scholarships, the coach was a local minister who had volunteered his time, and the baseball field was only one step better than playing on a cow pasture. Making the team was easy enough; losing game after game to virtually every team we played—including some junior colleges—was demoralizing. I loved the game too much to quit, but baseball was not going to provide the boost to my morale I had hoped it would.

Fortunately, the student-recruiting job had just the opposite effect. Each weekend, I checked out an available automobile from the college's limited pool and made appointments to see high school seniors who lived in Central Oklahoma. As I enlightened them and their parents about the merits of attending Oklahoma Christian College, I resold myself on what a good decision I had made in transferring from SMU.

"We have small classes and get tons of personal attention from the professors," I told Sondra Flynn and her parents one evening in their upscale home in northwest Oklahoma City. Sondra was a bright, beautiful young lady who could have gone to any college in Oklahoma. She was definitely leaning toward OCC, and my job was to close the sale.

"You're going to love dorm life," I gushed, "and the campus buildings are sleek and modern." That was my euphemistic way of saying, "small and utilitarian."

"What's social life like?" Sondra asked. "Is there much dating?"

Now, she had put me on the spot. My social life was pathetic, but then that was not characteristically true of my fellow classmates. So I covered the best I could.

"Unbelievable," I heard myself say as if I had dates five nights a week. "You'll be very popular from the day you hit campus." Within a few minutes, I had Sondra's signature on the form and her $10 application fee.

As the weeks progressed, student applications for the fall semester began to rise. Vice President Watson invited Jerry Wheeler to be a second student recruiter, responsible for the northern counties in Oklahoma and all of Kansas. I was assigned the southern counties and Texas. As charter members of "the dollar-an-hour club," Jerry and I became very good friends.

"Have you heard the latest?" Jerry asked one afternoon as we met in the tiny admissions office on the second floor of the science building.

"No. What's up?" I replied.

"Watson wants us to go with him on the chorale's spring break trip to Colorado," Jerry informed me. "He plans to raise money while you and I meet with high school students."

For a small, relatively unknown institution of higher education, Oklahoma Christian College had established a few outstanding programs that compared favorably to those offered at larger and more prestigious universities. At the top of the short list was OCC's *a capella* chorale. It was remarkable, one of the best I had ever heard.

Harold Fletcher was an assistant professor of music and the talented chorale's esteemed director. He had the distinction of having been the first faculty member hired by the college when it began operations in Bartlesville, Oklahoma, in 1950. His students thought he had no peer.

Each spring, Fletcher took his chorale on a tour of small towns and large cities within the college's limited sphere of influence. Concerts were held at churches and schools where old friends confirmed their warm feelings for the college and new friends were introduced to forty of its best ambassadors of goodwill. By the end of the week, I had thoroughly bought in to the idealism of

Christian higher education. This is where I belonged, and I was committed to bringing as many others as I could to the little college on the Oklahoma prairie.

SHELL KNOB

After completing final exams in mid-May, I was ready for a break from everything having to do with college. In fact, I was actually excited about my summer job in Springfield. Forget the dollar-an-hour position on campus; I was about to become a Swift and Company sales representative earning $200 per week.

Bob Nave, a stocky man in his mid-forties, with a full head of wavy blonde hair, was the manager of a new Swift and Company sales unit, designed to service hotel, restaurant, and institutional accounts in Southwest Missouri. He had hired my mother to be his office assistant and subsequently had asked me to run vacation routes and to open new accounts in the booming lake country, south of Springfield. I couldn't wait to get started.

"Good morning, ace," Mr. Nave said cheerfully as I made my first appearance in his office. "Are you ready for a new adventure?"

I assured him that I was and thanked him for making the job available to me.

"All right, then. I want you to meet the men who are responsible for filling your orders," Mr. Nave said as he led me through a small hallway and into the coolers at the back of the office complex.

The coolers were filled with thick cardboard boxes containing all kinds of meat products—Swift Premium Bacon, Swift Butterball Turkeys, Swift Premium Hostess Hams, and lunchmeats of every kind. Hanging at the back of the chilly room were USDA choice beef sides and beef rounds, ready to be cut to order for the restaurants that needed strip steaks, filets, or rib-eyes to satisfy their hungry customers.

"This is Johnny," Mr. Nave said, introducing me to a tough-looking man wearing a blood-smeared white apron and a white cap. "He has forgotten more about meat than you will learn this summer."

I started to extend my hand but realized Johnny was wearing gloves. They were also covered with blood, and the butcher snickered as he saw my embarrassment.

"Make sure I can read your writing," Johnny said curtly as he turned to walk away. "I don't want to have to cut out steaks for you more than once per order."

It appeared obvious that the men in the cooler were not going to become my best friends—at least not until I proved that I could handle my end of the working relationship.

Then Mr. Nave took me outside and into the parking lot where he showed me a brand new, 1962 sky-blue Ford Falcon with company lettering painted on the side. "This one is yours for the summer," the boss beamed. "It's a stick shift and doesn't have air-conditioning, but it will get you where you need to go. Just keep it serviced and let me know if you have any problems. You can take it home at night and on weekends, but keep your personal use to a minimum."

I was flabbergasted. A brand new car and it was mine to drive for the summer. What a sweet job this was going to be.

On a Missouri map, Mr. Nave laid out the routes he wanted me to travel. "Remember, your primary job is to open new accounts," Mr. Nave said emphatically. "Stop at any restaurant, school, or small grocery you pass along the highway. Spend some time visiting with the owners or the cooks that place the meat orders, especially those who work in Branson and all the little towns near the lakes. Then make the sale."

The first couple of weeks passed with modest results. I opened some accounts, but the orders were so small that it hardly justified the delivery truck driver making a stop on his semi-weekly rounds. The challenge was to increase the orders each week, and that began to happen as the owners grew more comfortable with our product line and our delivery schedule.

One day, I took a road that was slightly off my normal route and found myself at the Epperly-Cupps General Store in Shell Knob, Missouri. The white wood-framed building had been around a few years and was in need of some repairs. Two gasoline pumps were located in the drive immediately in front of the building. Knowing these kinds of stores carried lunchmeats, bacon, and hams, I stopped to get acquainted with the owner.

"Yes, I'm the owner," said Isaac Epperly, an elderly man with a winsome smile. "What can I do for you?"

We talked business for ten or fifteen minutes, and then I asked, "Would you happen to be related to Ida Epperly who lives in Oklahoma City?"

"Sure am," he replied. "She's my sister-in-law. How do you know her?"

"Well, I attend Oklahoma Christian College, and Mrs. Epperly is the receptionist in our administration building," I answered.

For a few minutes, I got an overview of the Epperly family tree. Then Mr. Epperly, assuming all male students at OCC were studying for the ministry, said, "Are you a preacher?"

"I've preached a few sermons," I answered tentatively.

"Do you see the little church building across the road?" Mr. Epperly nodded toward the front door. "Why don't you drive down on Sunday morning and preach for us? We can't pay much, maybe $25 a week, unless the contribution isn't that much, then we would pay you whatever's in the collection basket."

Shell Knob church building

Shell Knob was almost an hour's drive from Springfield, and the road curved up and down and all around the Ozark foothills. But my weekends weren't committed elsewhere, so I told Mr. Epperly I would be there the next Sunday morning, ready to preach. The experience might tell me something about whether I really wanted to pursue the ministry as a career choice. As the old saying goes, "Nothing ventured, nothing gained."

Shell Knob

The next Sunday was a beautiful summer's day in the Ozarks. Mr. Nave had given me permission to use the Falcon to make the trip to Shell Knob, and I had filled its gas tank before making my journey south. With windows rolled down, the spirited little Ford hugged the curved roads as if it were on tracks.

Sunshine blanketed fields of alfalfa, and Black Angus cattle grazed on the nutritious grass up and down the rocky hillsides. Mulling over some passages from my English literature class, I recalled Robert Browning's line, "God's in his Heaven—All's right with the world!" I kept one eye on the relatively light morning traffic and another on my sermon notes as I whisked through the state and county roads. A generation or two ago, a visiting preacher would have made a similar trip on horseback.

As I approached the little white-framed church, I saw three or four cars already parked on the expansive lawn adjacent to the building. Two other families, apparently living nearby, were making their way to the assembly hall by foot. Three grade-school boys were playing tag in the front yard, so I paused and introduced myself to them and learned they were Mr. Epperly's grandsons.

"Are you the preacher?" David Cupps said with a mischievous grin.

"I am for today," I replied.

"Well, I hope you don't preach too long because me and my brothers are going water skiing this afternoon," he informed me in very clear terms.

I patted him on the shoulder and gave him the assurance he wanted. "It'll be a short sermon. You can count on that."

Mr. Epperly and his son-in-law, John Cupps, greeted me at the front door and ushered me inside to meet their friends and neighbors. More than half of those assembled that morning were related to Mr. Epperly by blood or marriage. Most were cordial, making me feel welcomed, but a few appeared wary, uncertain that anyone my age could possibly know enough about the Scriptures to present a doctrinally sound sermon.

Immediately before the worship service was to begin, Mr. Epperly gave me a gentle warning regarding one of their members.

"There's one lady who is having some emotional problems," he said to me in quiet, confidential tones. "She may speak out in the middle of your sermon, and almost every time we offer an invitation, she will come to the front asking for prayers. When this happens, don't worry about it. We'll take care of the matter." He didn't identify the woman in the audience, leaving me to guess who my respondent for the morning might be.

By the time we had finished our third hymn, the last of the latecomers had arrived. We had, according to my best count, thirty-nine in attendance, and that included a baby quietly napping on her mother's lap. John Cupps, who had led the praise service, announced that we would sing "Just as I Am" as an invitation song at the close of the sermon. It was time for me to give it my best effort.

"This morning, I want us to look at some lessons we can learn from the life of Peter," I began my well-rehearsed opening line. From there the sermon followed three principal points drawn from the Scriptures and a few current illustrations to make the lesson relevant for the audience.

Each time I made eye contact with those seated in the pews, I wondered when the mystery lady would reveal herself. It was my good fortune that the interruption never occurred. One energetic wasp did take a couple of nose-dives in my direction, causing me to use my Bible as a shield, but the woman was neither seen nor heard.

That is, we did not hear from her until we sang the invitation song; and then, just as Mr. Epperly had said, here came a heavyset woman, waddling down the center aisle, wearing a pink-patterned cotton dress. She sat heavily on the front pew. I hesitated a moment, waiting for someone to handle the situation, but when Mr. Cupps concluded the last stanza of the hymn and asked the audience to be seated, I sat down next to the woman and waited for the local leaders to do whatever they deemed appropriate under these circumstances. I waited... and I waited... and I waited.

Suddenly, I felt a tap on my shoulder. Turning around, I saw Mr. Epperly, who whispered to me, "This isn't the one." The lady seated next to me, obviously not the mystery woman, had recently moved into the area and wanted to join the fellowship of the Shell Knob church. With considerable embarrassment, I announced her wishes to the congregation, and Mr. Epperly led the dismissal prayer.

That was the first of many Sundays spent in Shell Knob. Different members took me home each week and fed me a steady diet of fried chicken, mashed potatoes, sliced red tomatoes, green beans from their own gardens, and all the homemade dinner rolls I could eat. On a few special occasions, I spent the afternoon water-skiing on Tablerock Lake with the Cupps family.

The summer had gone especially well in the Ozarks, but it soon would be over and I would be returning to the college campus. Preaching or law? I was still undecided about a career path. An undergraduate degree in English, however, would allow me to keep both options open. That was one piece of the puzzle now in place.

THE DOUBLE DATE

"**P**ile in," I insisted to a crowd of students waiting for rides to the Sunday night services at the Village Church of Christ. For the first time since I was licensed to drive, I had my own car. It wasn't the red Corvette that boys my age dreamed of owning, but it was Mom and Dad's hand-me-down 1955 turquoise and black Plymouth sedan equipped with four wheels and six cylinders, and I wasn't too proud to drive it.

"Is there enough room for us too?" pleaded a couple of freshmen girls.

"Sure! We'll make room," I beamed as four students crammed into the back seat and two others sat next to me on the bench seat in front. Last year I had been dependent on rides from other students or from faculty members who drove the eighteen-mile round-trip from the Village to the Oklahoma Christian College women's residence halls' parking lot and then repeated the route, returning the students to campus after services. This year was going to be different. I was a free man; I had my own wheels!

1955 Plymouth Belvedere

The Village church was a popular choice among OCC students. James Kinney, the pulpit minister who hailed from Tennessee, had a warm, engaging personality and was especially friendly to the college students.

He and his wife, Brownie, had three sons and the eldest, Jim, Jr., was a sophomore at OCC. The Kinney's, along with a dozen other couples at the Village, went out of their way to feed us on Sunday nights and entertain us in their homes.

Tonight was like almost any other Sunday night at the Village. Mr. Kinney was preaching on autopilot to a half-filled auditorium, including some sleepy-headed college students scattered throughout the audience. The minister, speaking in his distinctive Southern drawl, was midway through his sermon when he decided to underscore one of his major points by singing a verse from a familiar hymn. Jim Lankford, a junior science major from Wichita, Kansas, was seated on the second row, soundly asleep. Hearing the preacher as he began to sing, Jim stirred to consciousness, and thinking it was time for the invitation song, he stood up and joined Mr. Kinney in an awkward duet. The entire audience worked hard to stifle a collective belly laugh.

After services, I bumped into Jim Kinney, Jr. in the hallway. "Can you believe Lankford?" Jim asked with a broad grin.

"Your dad really caught him off guard." I chuckled.

"Have you got a minute?" Jim inquired in a much more serious tone of voice.

"Sure," I replied, "but I do have a full load of students in my car, and I need to get them back to campus right away."

"Listen," Jim said rather nervously. "I want you to work on some songs with me and my brother, Ray. You know that Ray and I both play the guitar. If we can put a performing group together, I can get us some invitations to sing at a few youth programs and banquets. All you have to do is sing. Are you game?"

"Let me think about that one," I said hesitantly. "I haven't done anything like that in a few years, and I'm not sure I have the time for it now."

"I'll call you," Jim said as I turned to go. "We can practice at my house, and I think I already know of a couple of gigs where we can play."

Over the next few weeks, Jim, Ray, and I practiced singing folk songs that were being played constantly on the local radio stations. Our repertoire included the familiar standards "Cotton Fields," "Tom Dooley," "Where Have All the Flowers Gone?" and, "Michael, Row the Boat Ashore." Dimly lit coffee houses had become the dating venue of choice for many American teenagers and young adults; there, budding young vocal artists sang these folk songs, making popular once again this old genre of music.

Jim played rhythm guitar, Ray played bass, and I contributed nothing but a marginal lead baritone voice. We sang for a few high school groups, a couple of banquets, and one college student party. Had we been any good, we might have stayed with the venture, but what became obvious was that we weren't ready for the big time, and I had too many other interests to pursue without chasing this rainbow.

The Village church had a large high school group, and occasionally the elders asked a few of the college students to teach the teenage Bible classes. I had volunteered for that assignment and found that I had some personal teaching skills that worked well with these students.

One weekend, Jim, Jr. and I agreed to chaperone the high school class's outing to Springlake, a local amusement park that had a great fun house and the best roller coaster I had ever ridden.

"These high school girls are too young for us," Jim said glumly as we strolled past the park's midway barkers who were enticing us to play their sucker games. "We need to check out some of the new girls at OCC. There are a couple of dolls in that freshman class."

I nodded to let him know I was listening.

"Tell you what!" Jim continued. "I'll ask someone out for next Friday night if you will."

"You're on," I said. "Where do you want to go?"

"Maybe a movie and then to grab a bite at the Split-T," Jim responded without a second's hesitation. "I'll drive," he said. "Let me know when you get your date."

The next Friday night, I asked a young lady who was working at the reception desk in the women's A dorm to call for my date and then waited alone in the corner of the lobby for her to appear. The room was sparsely furnished with inexpensive chairs, a few tables and lamps, and two overstuffed sofas. A small black and white television sat at one end of the room, where two couples were watching a silly game show.

Men were allowed in the women's residence hall lobby only at certain hours of the week. Friday and Saturday nights were considered date nights, but curfew was eleven p.m. on Friday and ten p.m. on Saturday so that everyone would get a good night's rest before Sunday morning worship services. All freshmen were required to double date, which explained why Jim had asked me to get a date tonight. He apparently had his eyes on one of the new freshmen girls.

Before my date arrived, Jim came bounding into the lobby, waved quickly in my direction, and made a beeline to the receptionist, asking her to call for his date. Then he joined me in the corner.

"Is Split-T all right with you?" Jim asked. The Split-T on North Western Avenue was not only the best hamburger stand in Oklahoma City, it was the place to be. Always crowded on the weekends, the Split-T catered to high school and college students but had an excellent trade among older patrons as well. The girls liked to go there to see who was there, and the guys liked to go there because the girls liked to go there, and they both liked the hamburgers.

"I'm always game for the Split-T," I responded. "Who's your date tonight?"

But before Jim could answer, Barbara Burton, my date for the evening, came into the lobby through the residents' private door.

"Hi," she said with little emotion. Barbara and I had been on a couple of dates earlier in the fall, but there was not much chemistry between the two of us.

She was a petite young lady who appeared to know what she was looking for, and I had the feeling that I was not at the top of her list.

The next coed to enter the lobby was a girl I had seen before but had never met. She was usually with some of the more popular freshmen girls and a pack of upperclassmen boys who had more social courage than I. After signing the checkout sheet at the receptionist's desk, she walked quickly in our direction.

"This is Martha Mitchell," Jim said, making the introduction to Barbara and me while almost smacking his lips.

Wow! Jim had done all right for himself. This blue-eyed doll from Anadarko, Oklahoma, could light up any room with her unbelievable smile. Dressed in an olive green jumper and a plaid, long-sleeved shirt, Martha had the look of those young girls who modeled for *Seventeen.* She wore little makeup but teased her hair into an attractive style that was at least twice the size of a normal hairdo. I thought she looked perfect in every way—well, every way except for the fact she was Jim's date that evening instead of mine.

We ate hamburgers and fries at the Split-T, saw some other couples from OCC, and then dropped in to a small coffee house near Classen Circle. There we listened to folk songs and drank hot apple cider, returning to campus well before curfew. Although the evening had been fun, no one would have mistaken it for a romantic event. There were smiles and hand squeezes, but no goodnight kisses—and maybe that was just as well. If Jim didn't choose to pursue Martha Mitchell, he may have opened the door for me. We would have to see about all of that in the weeks ahead.

MARKING TIME

"Take out a half sheet of paper," instructed Professor Hugo McCord, "and number one to five." It was time for another pop quiz in my Hebrews class. Dr. McCord, fifty-something and almost always wearing a bow tie, was a meek soul who loved to teach the Bible classes at Oklahoma Christian College. He had tried administrative roles but had decided that he was not well suited for those assignments. His heart was in the classroom.

In three semesters, I had taken four of Dr. McCord's Bible courses, learning as much from observing his Christian demeanor as I had from what he taught us in his lectures. I had come to believe that professors at OCC truly cared about young people and that they made themselves available to students almost anytime, day or night. That impressed me.

"That's what Guy told me," Jerry Wheeler said as we walked out of the Hebrews class together. "McCord spent the night in his campus office because he heard about the blizzard that was supposed to hit Oklahoma City this morning. He was afraid he wouldn't be able to drive on the icy streets, and he didn't want to miss this class."

And Dr. McCord wasn't the only professor to make sacrifices on behalf of the students. My roommate had told me that Dr. Hugh McHenry, a math and science professor, had been in the men's residence halls at late hours the week before last, helping some of the physics students with their assignments. These instructors practiced the Christian principles that they taught in their classrooms. Amazing!

As I approached the midway point in my junior year, answers to some of my "life choice" questions began to emerge. I was much more confident about my decision to attend Oklahoma Christian College and had determined that I would finish an undergraduate bachelor-of-arts degree in English at OCC with a double minor in history and Bible. The ultimate career path was still somewhat fuzzy with law, ministry, and an indefinable role in higher education all in contention.

My social life was still limping along, but I knew I was playing in the right league. Having a car, I found it much easier to ask someone to dinner and a movie or to some other special event. The challenge continued to be in finding "Miss Right."

"They did what?" I cried, insisting that Jim Kinney, Jr. repeat what he had just said.

"You heard me right," Jim replied. "Elaine Russell, Marty Smith, and Martha Mitchell scaled the wall at the women's residence hall last weekend and spent the night out on the town. They crawled back over the wall in the wee hours of the morning. The whole thing is supposed to be hush-hush."

"Do you know where they went or what they could possibly have been doing all night?" I probed, allowing my curiosity to get the best of me.

"I'm not sure about any of that," Jim said with a shrug. "I think it was just a girls' night out on the town. Someone said they may have gone to a dance in Anadarko, but if they did, they didn't spend the night there."

"What were they thinking?" I said, trying to make sense of such a risky caper. "Don't they realize they could be sent home for a stupid trick like that?"

"I know," Jim said. "It's making me reconsider whether I want to ask Martha out again. She may be in a faster lane than the one I want to travel. Besides, I think she and Yamie McCown have become a steady item. They're together all the time."

Jim was right about Martha. I had seen her many times on campus, holding hands with James "Yamie" McCown. He was a playmaker guard for OCC's intercollegiate basketball team, the Eagles, and he appeared to be a playmaker with the girls too. From what I had observed, Yamie had sewed up the deal with the freshman coed from Anadarko.

In addition to my job as a student recruiter, I was also a residence hall assistant for the recently completed men's B dorm. There was always something going on in the residence halls. My job was to keep a lid on the everyday monkey business and take any serious breaches of the campus rules to my adult supervisor, Van Barnes.

"I have no idea who put it there," I informed Mr.

Barnes. "When I came to the lobby this morning, there it sat."

Actually, I thought the whole matter was a bit funny. Some gremlins had managed to roll a Volkswagen beetle into the lobby of the men's residence hall during the early morning hours, and there it was, a monument to their witty idea and their stealth in bringing it about.

"When you make the rounds tonight, see if you can pick up anything from some of the guys," Mr. Barnes directed me.

"All right," I replied, "but I'll be surprised if anyone's talking."

Curfew check was a mixed bag. Some residents were annoyed by my checking to see that they were in their rooms at curfew; others were glad for the intrusion and wanted to talk my ears off. As long as the men were in their rooms, it made little difference to me whether they were studying, sleeping, or playing a hot hand of Rook.

"Look who's here," Guy Ross said as I peeked inside his room. Although I had no idea who rolled the Volkswagen into the dorm lobby, if I had to guess, it would have been someone from this four-room suite.

Guy Ross

Earlier in the fall, Guy and some upperclassmen had tricked a freshman into thinking it was six a.m. and time for him to report for his student job in the cafeteria. In fact, it was only three a.m. Gremlins, again, had changed the freshman's alarm clock and his wristwatch. He had stood outside the cafeteria door for almost an hour, waiting for lights to come on and his shift to begin, before realizing something was wrong.

"Just checking for curfew," I said.

"We're all here," Guy assured me. "And you're just in time for our main event. Do you want to wrestle Parrish or Mansfield?"

Marvin Parrish and Mike Mansfield were two of Guy's suitemates and partners with him in tomfoolery. Mattresses were spread across the floor, and a small crowd was gathering at the door. The madmen of the midway were about to get this show underway.

"Thanks, but I'll pass tonight," I said, marking Guy and the others *present and accounted for* on my clipboard sheet. "Keep the noise level down or Barnes may be up here himself to knock a few heads."

I checked a few more rooms, satisfying myself that all men were at least on the premises, and then headed for Jerry Wheeler's room. There wouldn't be any wrestling going on in his suite. Jerry was serious about his studies and spent ample time with the books.

Jerry was propped up at one end of his bed, reading a commentary on the Apostle Paul's prison epistles. His glasses were as thick as Coke bottle bottoms, and the room was not very well lit. I could only wonder how he was able to read the tiny print in the tome he held in his hands.

"What's up?" he asked as I sat down on the hard-back chair near his desk.

"Something's bothering me," I began, not certain that I wanted to pursue this issue.

"Shoot," Jerry responded as he took off his glasses and rubbed his weary eyes.

"Have you heard about some freshman girls scaling the wall and spending the night out on the town this past weekend?" I said. Since Jim had told me this story, I had thought about nothing else all day. Normally, I wouldn't have cared that much, but for some reason, I couldn't turn this one loose.

"Yeah, I know one of them was Elaine Russell." Jerry smiled. "If I could get my nerve up, I would ask her to the Christmas banquet."

"You mean you would still be interested in dating a girl who did a stupid thing like that?" I said, sensing that I may have been overreacting.

"Sure! Why not?" Jerry shot back. "I think it's funny they could pull off the escape without encountering the night watchman or waking the dorm parents. They get high marks for raw courage in my book."

That night I slept a little better. Jerry helped me to realize that being a scholar, as he was and as I aspired to be, did not mean a person had to take himself too seriously, closing all of the doors that are marked "fun and games." Cars in the lobby, wrestling matches in the dorm rooms, and occasionally scaling a wall to spend the night on the town were all part of growing from adolescence into adulthood. There are those times when a student needs to take off his scholarly mask that says, "I am boring," and have some uninhibited fun in his life. Sweet dreams.

SPRING, GLORIOUS SPRING

Oklahoma Christian College may have lacked something in not having intercollegiate football, but it compensated for the loss by fielding outstanding basketball teams and track squads for the enjoyment of its students and many fans. The common denominator attributable to OCC's success in both sports was a dedicated coach named Ray Vaughn. OCC had recruited the highly acclaimed coach from his comfortable position at Capitol Hill High School and had installed him as its first coach and athletic director on its new Oklahoma City campus.

For the first few years, Coach Vaughn led the track and basketball programs, excelling in both. The men's relay teams competed commendably in major track and field meets held on large NCAA university campuses, while the basketball team surprised many of the better known colleges in Oklahoma, winning four out of every five games they played. Eventually, the burden of recruiting, training, and coaching in both fields became too much, and Coach Vaughn passed the basketball reins to Haskell Sinclair, a much younger coach from Abilene, Texas. Among those players whom Coach Sinclair brought with him was James "Yamie" McCowan.

Yamie was fun to watch on the basketball court. He was quick and energetic, capable of stealing the ball from his opponent, dribbling it between his legs, pushing the play down the court, and then passing the ball behind his back to a teammate who was trailing him to the basket. He was also an excellent shooter. It was an exceptional night when he did not score in double digits.

Basketball game in the Barn

"Can you believe he can do that?" Jerry Wheeler exclaimed as Yamie dribbled the basketball through five stunned players from John Brown University.

"He's incredible," I concurred. "Where does he come up with those moves?"

The Eagles were having their way with JBU that night. The game was being played in a large metal building, affectionately known as "the Barn." Eight rows of bleachers along the north wall of the building held the boisterous student body and a few dozen boosters who came faithfully to each contest to see the Eagles play their running, gunning style of basketball.

All of a sudden, something in the bleachers caught my eye. *Is that Charles Cosgrove sitting next to Martha Mitchell?* Sure enough, it was. Something must have happened between her and Yamie.

Charles was a junior Bible major and a recognized leader among his classmates. Although a decent student, his long suit was humor; he loved to make people laugh. Everything I had heard was that girls found humor to be charming, and there he was, charming the bobby socks off of that unsuspecting freshman from Anadarko.

Martha sat next to Charles, but at a respectable distance. I would give her good marks for that. But judging by her smile and bright flashing eyes, she was enjoying Charles's wit and flirtatious humor a bit too much. She wore a crimson red, full skirt with a cream-colored sweater. Her hair was teased and shaped in a beehive. And that smile—I couldn't get over that smile.

Unable to keep my eyes off the couple seated twenty feet to my right and three rows down, I hardly watched a moment of the game in the second half. By the end of the game, I knew that we had won but could not have told you how we managed to get the job done. My mind was a thousand miles away.

The next day at baseball practice, I sought out Mike Gipson, a freshman pitcher from Jonesboro, Arkansas. Mike played baseball and basketball. He might know the scoop on Yamie and Martha.

"Good game last night," I said as I approached Mike near the third base bench. "Two more weeks of basketball left?" I inquired.

"That's about it," Mike said as he began his pre-practice stretching exercises.

"Let me ask you something," I said, stumbling for the right words. I decided the best course was to get the matter squarely on the table. "Are James McCown and Martha Mitchell still dating one another?"

"Depends," he replied. "I don't think they're dating each other exclusively, but I know Yamie likes her a lot." Mike stopped his toe-touching exercise and looked at me with a sheepish grin. "Are you thinking about making a pass at her? Huh?" He broke out laughing. "Go for it, but don't tell him I told you."

As I approached the women's residence hall lobby, I felt butterflies in the pit of my stomach—the kind you get just before playing a championship game. The debate in my mind had been whether to call Martha and ask her for a date or just show up in the lobby. I had decided on the latter. There was always the risk of her turning me down on the phone, but if she came to the lobby when I called for her, we could take matters from there. Besides, it was a Thursday night, not an official date night.

The receptionist in the lobby of women's A dorm was a red-haired junior who stayed up with all the social life on campus. Once I called for Martha, the word would be out and spread through all quarters of the women's dorms before morning.

"Excuse me," I said as nonchalantly as I knew how. "Would you call for Martha Mitchell?"

The redhead paused for a moment as if she didn't hear me clearly and then began smacking her bubblegum and reached for the intercom switch to Martha's suite. "Martha Mitchell, there's someone to see you in the lobby," she said.

After a few seconds passed, I heard Martha ask, "Who is it?"

"It's a guy," the receptionist responded as if to shroud the moment in mystery.

"Just a minute," came the reply, slightly garbled over the primitive intercom system.

I waited four or five minutes, each one seeming like an eternity. One other couple sat in a sofa watching the television. I nodded their way and smiled. Two of the cheerleaders came bouncing into the lobby, looked momentarily in my direction, and moved on to the door that led to the residents' rooms. I stood there rehearsing my opening line so many times that it began to sound stale.

Finally, Martha appeared at the door. Dressed in a corduroy jumper and a navy blue blouse, she looked like every boy's dream. If she saw me as she entered the lobby, she must have assumed that her suitor was someone else. She walked quickly past me, toward the receptionist's counter and inquired, "Who called for me?"

The receptionist gestured with an open hand in my direction. Martha turned, smiled that million-dollar smile, and said, "Oh, hi! I didn't know it was you."

"I don't mean to interrupt your study time, but I wondered if you would like a break to get a Coke at the student center?" I barely managed to get the words out.

She paused for a second and then said, "Sure, I'd love to. Let me get a jacket."

We walked slowly up the terraced esplanade that led to the student center. A small grill operated each evening for those students who had missed their meal in the cafeteria or wanted a late night snack. My favorite treat at the grill was the Frito pie, but I would pass on it tonight because I didn't want to take any chances eating onions.

"How about a Coke?" I said, looking to Martha for her approval.

"Sounds great," she responded, flashing her awesome smile.

"We'll have two Cokes," I said to the student who was operating the grill.

I paid twenty cents for the sodas, and we found a small, round table with armless, straight-back chairs where we sat and began to get acquainted. If she was nervous in the least, she didn't show it. I wanted to talk to her all night, but curfew was in twenty minutes.

We strolled back to the women's residence halls

without holding hands or having any physical contact with one another. I wanted to grab her by the shoulders and plant a Hollywood-style kiss right on her lips, as if to claim her as my own personal property. That's what Clark Gable would have done, but this wasn't Hollywood, and I was certainly not Clark Gable. I settled for lightly touching her shoulder as I opened the door to the residence hall lobby.

"Are you available Saturday night?" I managed to ask before telling her goodnight.

"I'm sorry," she said, "but I already have a date for Saturday."

This was not going to be a cakewalk, but my resolve to see her again was even greater than when the night began.

"I'll call you," I promised, "and maybe we can work out another time." We said our good-byes, and I watched her as she disappeared behind the door leading to the coeds' private living quarters. This wasn't exactly the type of date you would describe as unforgettable, but then again, perhaps it was.

THIS MAGIC MOMENT

For the past three days, I had been recruiting high school seniors in the Dallas area for Oklahoma Christian's 1963–64 freshman class. Surprisingly, I had found considerable interest south of the Red River and had picked up eight applications for admission accompanied by the mandatory $10 deposit fee. Three more prospects were likely to sign before my return to Oklahoma. It had been a very profitable trip.

Since transferring to OCC, I hadn't seen any of my Phi Delt brothers from SMU. Having an extra hour to kill, I decided it would be fun to drop by fraternity row and see if any of my former Phikeia brothers were hanging out at the Phi house. I parked my car at the curb in front of the house, walked to the front door, and felt a little shiver of anxiety as I recalled the hazing that had occurred almost every time I set foot inside this house.

Immediately upon opening the door, I sensed a buzz of activity. A three-piece band was setting up in the corner of the formal room, and furniture was being moved against the walls, allowing space for a dance.

"Looks like you're getting ready for a mixer," I said to a young man wearing a Phikeia emblem tacked firmly onto his blue button-down Oxford shirt.

"Yes, sir," he replied. "The Pi Phi's are coming over in about an hour. Are you looking for someone?"

I explained to him that I had been in his shoes two years ago but now lived in Oklahoma. "Would Jim Harris be around?" I asked.

"He's rarely here in the daytime," the freshman said "but he may show up for the party. You're welcome to wait."

"Thanks," I said. "I'll look around and see who's still here that I know. Oh, by the way, is there a pay phone I can use?"

"Yes sir! Just around the corner and down the hall on your left," the young man answered and then continued moving some furniture away from the center of the room.

The house was practically empty in the residence hall wings. Most of the brothers were either still in class or participating in an intramural softball game against their next-door neighbors, the Phi Gams. I found the telephone booth and sat down to make a long-distance call to the Oklahoma Christian campus. Dr. Baird wanted to hear about my visit with Tom Milholland, a Dallas high school senior whose mother was secretary at the Skillman Avenue church.

"Dr. Baird, please," I said when his office assistant answered the ring. A minute or two passed when the president picked up the line.

We chatted briefly, and then I said, "I thought you might like an update . . ."

Before I could get the words out of my mouth, the band that was scheduled to play for the mixer in the next room began practicing its rendition of "Louis, Louis" in thunderous tones and a pounding bass beat. I couldn't hear myself think, much less carry on a conversation. The only thought running through my mind was, *What will Dr. Baird think? He probably imagines that I'm calling from some honky-tonk on the wrong side of town.*

Recruiting wasn't the only thing on the upswing this spring. Baseball was decidedly better than the year before. Haskell Sinclair, who had been hired principally to coach basketball, was also the new baseball coach. He approached the assignment professionally, scheduling a full complement of games, and put us through enough preseason conditioning to make us feel as if we were going to be competitive.

Mike Gipson, only a freshman, was our ace on the mound. We weren't deep in any position but had enough talent to win a few more games than we had the year before. There were no seniors in the starting line-up, and I was the only junior; all of the other starters were either freshmen or sophomores.

"Let's go right after practice is over," Mike said as we finished running sprints in the outfield.

"Are you sure it's today?" I asked.

Mike Gipson

"That's what I heard in chem class," he responded. "Powder-puff football on the intramural field at five p.m., and they should be underway about now."

Suddenly, a whistle blew. Coach Sinclair assembled us near the pitching mound, gave us some instructions regarding the game we were to play the next day against Langston University, and sent us on our way. Mike and I grabbed our gear and began jogging toward the rough, uneven fields east of the baseball diamond. There we found a small crowd of students cheering on the two teams of girls who were playing powder-puff flag football. It was a riot.

Making the spectacle all the more entertaining was watching Martha Mitchell run up and down the field in hot pursuit of Archie Wright's flag. Wearing rolled-up blue jeans, a gray short-sleeved sweatshirt and blue and white sneakers, Martha looked like a doll off the toy shop's top shelf. She even played football wearing a smile.

"Come on, Martha!" I yelled. "Don't let her turn the corner!" She paused just long enough to look in my direction as if to say, *If you think it's so easy, get yourself out here and give it a try.*

After the game, I worked my way past a few fans and well-wishers to find Martha. She was laughing with friends, enjoying the moment.

"You looked good out there," I said, meaning it in more ways than one.

"Thanks," she replied. "I didn't know you were going to be here."

"Mike told me about it," I said "or I might have missed it." Then with a little more caution in my voice, I asked, "Any chance you'd be available to go to the movies this Friday night?"

I had seen Martha on campus a few times since our Coke date two weeks ago, but I hadn't been able to get my name on her date book. She had a busy social life with multiple suitors standing in line. At least the stranglehold with Yamie had been broken. If I had any chance to build a relationship with her, it needed to be now.

"I'm pretty sure Friday night is open," she said.

"Great!" I beamed. "Let's say six o'clock. I'll call for you in the lobby."

We walked together to the women's residence hall where I told Martha good-bye and floated on air all the way back to my dorm room.

Friday night, I splashed a little extra after-shave tonic on my face and headed for the women's dorm. At the risk of getting Martha and me both in trouble, I had suggested we ignore the rule about freshmen having to double date. She readily agreed. We both thought it was a stupid rule and were willing to pay the consequences if we got caught.

Shirley Jones, Gig Young, and Red Buttons starred in *A Ticklish Affair,* a romantic comedy that set the mood for the rest of the evening. Following the movie, we ate a pizza at Sussy's on North Lincoln Boulevard and then drove back to campus. A few couples were in the middle of steamy embraces in cars parked at the dormitory lot, but I was pretty sure we weren't ready for that.

"Let's take a walk," I suggested, hoping that she would be open to the idea of spending a few more minutes with me. The moon was full and the temperature mild as we meandered down the sidewalk that led from the residence halls to the Barn. Gas lights lined the walk creating an amber glow, and as we crossed the campus road and walked toward the baseball field, I reached for her hand.

Martha asked about baseball and where my interest in the game had begun—a question whose answer could have taken me hours to unfold. I abbreviated my response and led her to home plate.

With my hands on her shoulders, I turned her to face the outfield where the moon, high in the sky, was a glorious sight. We stood there, saying nothing to each other for a minute or more; then, as if on cue, I turned her around, facing me, and leaned down for a well-intentioned kiss. She responded as I had hoped she would, and it was a magical moment. Her lips were soft and moist, tasting like honey.

What a beautiful night. I had made my move and had found no resistance. We agreed to spend more time with one another for the remaining few weeks of the semester. This was a relationship that could have a bright future. I was determined to keep the line tight, not giving Martha any reason to slip off the hook.

BLACK WEDNESDAY

The summer had been as long and hot as the movie starring Paul Newman and Joanne Woodward. I had spent my second year working for Mr. Nave, opening new accounts for Swift and Company throughout Southwest Missouri, and had preached each Sunday for the Shell Knob church. I made one trip to Arkansas to see Martha who worked as a lifeguard at Camp Wyldewood near Searcy. As far as I could determine, the flame was still lit on our budding romance.

Student recruiting this past year had been so terrific that Oklahoma Christian College relaxed its rule requiring all students to live in campus housing. This fall, senior men would be permitted to live with certain families who had opened their homes to accommodate the expected overflow. Jerry Wheeler and I had been approved in the program and were assigned to live with the Marion Hickingbottom family, residing one block south of the campus.

Jerry arrived in Oklahoma City two days earlier than I, moving in with the Hickingbottoms on Monday. I waited until Wednesday, the day prior to first-day classes, before leaving home to commence my senior year. The Plymouth and I hauled onto campus in the early afternoon, and with no air-conditioning, both of us were running on fumes.

From the admissions office, I made a quick telephone call to Martha, telling her that I was on campus and would be in her residence hall lobby at 6:15 p.m. This would give us ample time to drive to the Village Church for mid-week services. The elders had asked me to be their part-time youth minister this fall, agreeing to pay me five dollars a week for gas money.

After a stop at the student center to see the new wing that had been under construction during the summer months and a brief visit to the bookstore to pick up three new textbooks, I drove to the Hickingbottom's house and pulled in next to Jerry's car that was parked in the driveway.

"Hey, man, I thought you might have decided not to come back," Jerry said as he answered the doorbell. The Hickingbottoms both worked and were not home. Jerry and I sat on the twin beds and got caught up with what had been going on the past few months. We were both excited about the fall and what we hoped to do during our senior year.

"Why don't you come with Martha and me to the Village tonight?" I asked.

"Can't," Jerry replied. "Watson's out of town and wants me to fill in for him at the church in Harrah. Mrs. Watson and their baby are going with me and two or three girls from Wichita. Phil wants me to see if we can get some of the college kids to attend Harrah during the school year, so I told him I'd give it a try."

"How long does it take to get there?" I asked, not knowing exactly how far it was from campus.

"It won't take much longer than your trip to the Village," Jerry answered. "Harrah is just a few miles east of Oklahoma City, but there's a back road that'll get you there in thirty minutes, or less."

Jerry Wheeler

I spent some time unpacking and showering before saying good-bye to Jerry and driving to campus for my date with Martha. She was every bit as beautiful as the image I had been dreaming of over the summer. We walked hand in hand to the parking lot, hopped into the fatigued sedan, and made our way to the Village. The fall was full of promise.

In lieu of classes, all adults, college students, and high school students met that evening for a special period of worship in the Village Church's new auditorium. Dr. Darvin Keck, an OCC science professor and one of the song leaders at the church, had asked me and some other college-age men to make brief comments from the Scriptures. It was an uplifting service and a personal joy for me to be sharing the moment with Martha.

With both of us needing some time to settle into our new quarters, Martha and I arrived back at the dorm an hour before curfew. I managed a goodnight kiss in the parking lot before walking her to the B dorm lobby. We agreed to meet each other the next morning for chapel, and I drove back to the Hickingbottoms. Jerry had not yet returned from Harrah.

As I finished unpacking some items from my footlocker and began perusing one of the textbooks I had purchased from the bookstore, I listened to the music being played by the disc jockeys on KOMA 1520 AM radio in Oklahoma City. There had been a subtle shift in the sound of pop music from the classic rock and roll of the 1950s to a new beat that was now popular with the teenagers. They were big into push dance music and the early sounds of the twist. Since leaving SMU, I had not kept up with the new dance crazes and was not a huge fan of the new musical artists.

It was now a few minutes past curfew, and I was surprised that Jerry was not home. Of course, he had to take Mrs. Watson and Angie home and then get the girls back to the dorms, but he should have been here by now. Perhaps he stopped by the men's dorm to see some of the guys.

"We interrupt this program for a news bulletin," the radio announcer said. "There has been a car-train crash, with fatalities, east of Oklahoma City tonight. Details are unavailable at this time, but as we learn more, we will keep you advised."

Bells began ringing in my head. *Did he say the accident had been east of Oklahoma City? Was this just a coincidence, or could there be something sinister in that news report?*

I couldn't think of any way to reach Jerry or check on his whereabouts, but then I remembered the Watsons. If Mrs. Watson was safely at home, this report could not have had anything to do with him or those who had travelled with him to Harrah. So I ran out the front door, jumped into my car, and drove to the Smiling Hill subdivision, north of campus, where the Phil Watson family resided.

The small brick home on Harding Avenue was dark except for the single outside light that illuminated the front porch. Turning into the Watson's driveway, I slammed on my brakes, sprang from the car, and ran to the front door. There, I rang the doorbell and prayed for a response. Fighting back tears, I rang the bell again. Nothing!

For a moment, I was unable to think of any sensible course of action. I didn't know how to reach Mr. Watson and didn't know what I would say to him if I did. My only option was to enlist some help from campus; so, I drove to the men's residence hall where I found a large gathering of male students seated on the floor in the lobby and engaged in a dorm meeting. My eyes scanned the faces of each student, satisfying myself that Jerry was not in the room.

Dr. Willis E. Kirk, the Dean of Students, was at the dorm to speak with the men regarding rules and regulations for the coming year.

"Excuse me, Dean Kirk," I interrupted, "but I have an emergency and need to speak with you immediately."

Sensing my panic, Dr. Kirk asked Tommy Williams, the new supervisor for the men's dorms, to take over the meeting while he and I stepped outside.

"Have you heard the news report about a car-train crash tonight?" I whispered loud enough to be heard ten feet away. "I'm afraid it may be some of our students."

I shared with Dr. Kirk everything I knew about Jerry's plans for the evening, the KOMA news bulletin, my inability to get a response at the Watson's house, and then begged him to help me get some answers. He stepped quickly into Mr. Williams' apartment that was adjacent to the lobby of the dormitory and made some telephone calls. When he returned, he said, "Is your car nearby?"

"In the back lot," I replied.

"Do you mind driving?" he said with some strain in his voice.

"Not at all," I said. "Let's go."

Dr. Kirk told me what he had learned from his telephone calls. According to the Oklahoma Highway Patrol, there had been a fatal accident and those who were involved had been taken to the hospital in Midwest City. He had an address, and we sped quickly to that location. Upon arriving in Midwest City, we were redirected to the Mercy Hospital on NW 10th Street in downtown Oklahoma City.

Dr. Kirk had made a second call to the women's residence hall where the receptionist had confirmed that three female students had not made curfew. Two were from Wichita, Kansas, and a third was from Albuquerque, New Mexico. No one had an explanation for their absences.

We arrived at Mercy Hospital just a few minutes before midnight and made our way to the emergency room entrance. A nurse listened patiently while Dr. Kirk identified himself and told why we were concerned. The RN stepped inside a room, and when she returned, a young medical doctor in scrubs was at her side.

After listening to our story, the doctor said, "Please, come with me."

He led Dean Kirk and me through some dimly lit hallways, through two sets of swinging double doors, and into a room that had to be unlocked with a key. I was totally unprepared for what I saw inside the room. Six lifeless bodies lay on pallets and gurneys, all bruised, cut and swollen, almost beyond recognition.

"Are you able to help us identify these individuals?" the young doctor asked in a quiet professional tone.

"This young man is more likely to recognize them than I," Dr. Kirk explained. "He knows most of the students."

Indeed, I did know five of those lying before me. Janice Novak, a junior, and Karen Hetrick, a sophomore, were both from Wichita. I knew Jacqulin Watson and presumed the small child was her daughter, Angie. And, of course, I knew Jerry. The only one I did not recognize was the third coed, who happened to be Sharon Stewart, a freshman from Albuquerque.

The longer I stood before the carnage, trying to fathom the atrocity of the moment, the more I became unable to stand at all. With tears streaming uncontrollably down my face, I fell to my knees next to Jerry's corpse and made a futile attempt to offer a silent prayer. There was no use to try. My brain was numb, my heart was broken, and I had no way of putting into words what I felt deep within my soul.

Dean Kirk was up the rest of the night making calls to family members, sharing with them the worst news they could ever have imagined. Four young people in the prime of life were snuffed out in an instant. A young mother and her precious child were never going to answer that doorbell again. And where had they been? To church—not some seedy hole on the bad side of town, but to church!

I didn't get much sleep that night. This was my first day to spend in an unfamiliar house, and the nightmarish events of the past few hours played out as a stream of consciousness, flooding my beleaguered mind with uncomfortable images. As I struggled with the convictions of my own faith, tears kept rolling onto my pillowcase. I begged God for answers and for daylight so that I would not have to endure this emotional trauma alone.

Jerry Wheeler's automobile
after the train collision

ON BENDED KNEES

The next morning, the sun rose right on schedule. I don't know why or how, but there it was as if nothing had occurred in the past twelve hours that called for its taking a day off. Sunglasses firmly in place to hide my red, bleary eyes, I drove over to the campus.

At first glance, everything appeared to be normal on the hill. Breakfast was being served in the cafeteria, faculty and staff were scurrying to their respective classrooms and offices, and students were making their way to early morning classes. I had already decided that I would not try to attend mine.

The flag in front of the student center was flying at half-mast, confirming that my remembrance of the night before was not a dream. Inside I found a small group of upperclassmen seated at a round table and reading the front-page article in *The Daily Oklahoman*.

"Can you believe that car?" Don Young said incredulously. A photo of Jerry's mangled Ford accompanied the newspaper's lead story for the day.

"They didn't have a chance," Guy Ross chimed in. "I hope they didn't suffer. I mean, that they didn't know what hit them."

All day, students and faculty chewed over the known facts and played the "why game." The administration spoke about the accident in chapel, offering spiritual words of comfort and announcing that a memorial service would be held Friday afternoon in the Barn. Tears flowed freely among students who were broken in spirit and were experiencing a collective loss of innocence.

I found Martha in the cafeteria during the noon hour. Without saying a word, she buried her head into my chest and cried tears of consolation. She was the only person who could extend comfort to me at that moment. We left the cafeteria arm in arm, bonding with one another in order to bear our mutual pain.

Early the next week, I received a telephone call from Phil Watson. Although he had just buried his wife and daughter and was functioning under enormous personal stress, he reached out to me, seeking to know how I was handling Jerry's death.

"What are you planning to do?" asked Mr. Watson. "Will you stay at the Hickingbottoms or move into the dorms?"

"I haven't decided for sure, but probably move into the dorms if I can find space," I replied.

"Why don't you pack up your things and move in with me?" Mr. Watson said, catching me totally off guard.

"Really? You wouldn't mind?" I said.

"No, I'm serious," Mr. Watson said. "I have two empty bedrooms. Can you cook?"

"I hope you're kidding," I said with a chuckle. "I don't even know how to scramble eggs."

The next few weeks were difficult to manage. Neither Mr. Watson nor I knew much about cooking or housecleaning. Classes were a drag, and I had lost my enthusiasm for student recruiting. Martha and I were constantly at each other's sides, but the social scene on campus languished in the shadow of the tragic accident. It was hard to have much fun without feeling guilty.

In early October, I agreed to take two Springfield students home for a quick weekend. We left immediately after classes on Friday and were hoping to be home before nine p.m. Somewhere near Big Cabin, Oklahoma, on the Will Rogers Turnpike, the old Plymouth threw a rod and ground to a noisy halt on the side of the road. There was nothing to do except call my dad.

"I don't know what it is," I explained to Dad. He was not in a pleasant mood.

"Well, stay where you are, and I'll bring something to tow you in," he said. "It'll take me two hours or more to get there."

Those were long hours, and so were the three hours it took Dad to tow me into Springfield. When we got home, however, he had worked through his frustration and was trying to come up with a plan to get me and my friends back to campus.

"The Dodge dealer has been running a television ad for their new Dart," Dad said. "Only $1,717 for a new one." I could hardly believe my ears.

"You mean I might be able to get a new car?" I said, more than pleading the case.

"We'll see in the morning," he replied.

Sunday afternoon, I drove a brand new, four-door

tan Dodge Dart back to Oklahoma City. It was the first time I had managed to have a legitimate smile on my face in the past five weeks. Upon arriving on campus, I dropped off my two passengers at the residence halls, picked up Martha, and took her for a spin.

"Guess what," she said, after we had exhausted the subject of how I got the new car.

"What?" I replied.

"I learned while you were gone that I'm on the ballot for homecoming queen," she said with a perky little smile. "Julie Smith, Jo Anderson, and me."

"And you're just a sophomore," I said, as if one or the other of us didn't know that already. "That's a good reason to celebrate. What about dinner at Sleepy Hollow next Friday night?"

Homecoming at Oklahoma Christian College, always filled with tradition, began with a huge bonfire on Friday night. Alumni chapel was scheduled for Saturday morning followed by a barbeque lunch in the cafeteria; then the annual homecoming basketball game was played in the Barn. At halftime, the queen candidates and class attendants were presented on center court immediately prior to the crowning of a new homecoming queen.

Martha looked as beautiful as any storybook princess in her long, white satin, sleeveless formal dress. Escorted by the student body vice president, Jerry Pospisil, she stood with the other two candidates, facing the packed bleachers and awaiting the highly anticipated announcement.

Martha at homecoming coronation

"And this year's Oklahoma Christian College homecoming queen is... Martha Mitchell!" the public address announcer said while the audience erupted into thunderous applause. Martha looked every bit the part of royalty.

The previous queen, Mary Parks, placed the tiara on Martha's head, and Jerry Pospisil leaned down for an opportunistic kiss, as if that was necessary to make the announcement official. I felt a surge of jealousy pulse through my whole body, and the thought filtered through my mind, *I may need to tie this filly down before someone else steals the reins.*

Two weeks later, the campus was brought to its knees once again. This time, it wasn't just a tempest in our little teapot, but an unspeakable tragedy that staggered the entire nation. President John F. Kennedy had been shot by an assassin's bullets in Dallas, Texas. We joined with fellow citizens throughout the world in mourning the loss of our nation's leader. Some of us on campus began to wonder if our season of grief would ever come to an end.

For the Thanksgiving break, Martha came to Springfield and met my family for the first time. Mom fixed the traditional turkey dinner, complete with dressing, mashed potatoes, green beans and beets from my dad's garden, and my grandmother's homemade candied apples. The meal was a big hit—and so was Martha.

The next day, I made a trip to Zale's Jewelry Store on the northeast corner of Springfield's downtown square. Shopping for an engagement ring was a totally new experience and one that made me more than a little nervous. The whole ordeal was made even more difficult by the fact that I only had $350 to spend. With help from a kind, sympathetic saleswoman, I found a beautiful wedding set on sale and made my purchase.

On Saturday afternoon, as Martha and I were returning to Oklahoma, I stopped the car on the side of the road. With the ring tucked firmly in my hand, I made an awkward, rather unromantic proposal of marriage. Apparently Martha didn't have any better offers because she said "yes," conditional upon her parents offering their blessing. Next stop: Anadarko!

FOREVER

I left Martha at her residence hall lobby one Friday night and walked across campus to my room in men's B dorm. Five months after the tragic car-train accident, Phil Watson married Mary Parks, who was teaching school in Washington, Oklahoma, and I was once again without a place to stay. Fortunately, Mary's brother Mac lived alone in the dorm, so the extra bed in his room was available for the balance of the spring semester.

Mac had made a trip to his home in Arkansas that weekend, and I found myself sitting on my bed and contemplating the magnitude of some decisions I had made over the past few months. The senior year was coming to a close, and I could see broad silver linings encircling those dark holes that had haunted me three years ago in Dallas.

The career path was not completely settled, but I had taken the LSAT exam, applied to SMU's College of Law, and had been accepted with a respectable scholarship for the fall. Corporate law still had some appeal, and there were other fields where a law degree might prove beneficial. I had not turned my back entirely on ministry, but had determined that a professional degree in law from a well-established university would open more doors in my future than spending three or four years in seminary studies. Another piece of the puzzle was coming into place.

Martha and I had set a wedding date of May 2, which happened to coincide with her parents' twenty-second wedding anniversary. The date was also three weeks before I was scheduled to receive my bachelor of arts in English from Oklahoma Christian College. I never had a doubt that Martha was the one person I wanted to marry and the woman who would be the ideal mother for my children. She was the love of my life.

There were other issues that had been favorably resolved over the span of two or three years. The adolescent religious faith that I had inherited from my parents and had brought with me to college had been examined in a much more thorough manner in my formal studies at OCC and in the everyday trials and tribulations of life. I now held to an adult faith that was the product of my own experiences, and I purposed to embrace those spiritual convictions openly as an adult.

When I looked back at what had happened in such a short period of time, it was apparent that the decision to transfer to Oklahoma Christian for my sophomore year was the pivotal factor in bringing my life into clearer focus. "God moves in a mysterious way," William Cowper had written, and I had come to believe it emphatically. The decisions may have been mine, but the circumstances that surrounded me were orchestrated by someone who knew more about me than I knew about myself.

If there was anything unpleasant in my life, it was that my years of playing organized baseball were coming to an end. I had carried on a love affair with the game for more than fifteen years. Baseball was part of my DNA.

My dream of playing professional baseball, once alive and optimistic about the future, had vanished while playing at Oklahoma Christian. It was painful to realize that this would be my last season to lace up the spikes, doff the cap, and assume a menacing stance in the batter's box. Rather than being a participatory activity, baseball was about to become my favorite spectator sport.

"Just five more games," Mike Gipson said as he and I took our practice-ending lap around the field. "Are you ready to hang 'em up?"

"Why not?" I responded. "This has been a tough year at the plate, and I have a lot of things on my mind right now besides baseball."

"Guess so," Mike said. "Can you believe a week from now you'll be an old married man, henpecked by your wife and answerable to a mother-in-law?" Mike was always helping me look at the "brighter" side of life, and he was also going to be one of my groomsmen at the wedding.

"Your day will come," I chided him, "and when it does, you remember your own words. By the way, the rehearsal dinner will be Friday night at the Black Beaver Restaurant in Anadarko."

The week had passed quickly, and now Martha and I were standing before two hundred guests who were witnessing the exchange of our vows. Dr. Darvin Keck, dressed in his Sunday-best dark suit and tie, officiated at the services. He was sweating profusely, often wiping his forehead with his handkerchief in the stuffy un-air-conditioned church building. *Why does he look so nervous?* I wondered as he labored over the vows. *I'm the one getting married!*

"I do," I heard myself say.

"I do," Martha said softly.

My brother Tim, who was my best man, handed me the ring, and I slipped it on Martha's finger.

"You may kiss the bride," Dr. Keck announced, and he didn't have to say it twice. We marched down the center aisle, husband and wife, and into the sunshine of marital bliss.

Wedding recessional - May 1964

A surprise guest at the wedding was Jim Harris, my Phikeia friend from SMU. I hadn't seen Jim in three years, but he had driven to Oklahoma to support Martha and me on this special occasion. In the early morning hours before the wedding, Jim and I had devised an escape strategy to thwart the chicanery planned by Martha's older brother Brooks.

"Anything I can do to help?" Jim had offered.

"As a matter of fact, there is," I replied. "Martha's brother Brooks is trying to get my car so that he can decorate it before we leave the reception. I don't want him to mess with it, but need a little assistance to foil his plans." Jim followed me out of town that morning, and we set up our counter attack to Brooks' mischievous scheme.

The reception was an outdoor event in the backyard of the Mitchells' next-door neighbors, Paul and Clara Keyes. Martha and I cut the cake, sipped the punch, and greeted scores of friends, family, and well-wishers who were baking in the afternoon sun. Meanwhile, Brooks was looking frantically for the getaway car, which he presumed would be my Dodge Dart.

After changing into her going-away dress and tossing her flowers to her sister Sarah, Martha was ready to join me in the big escape. Brooks and a few of his pals had finally figured out that Jim Harris was going to drive us away in his car. They created a car caravan behind Jim's Chevy, honking their horns and promising to follow us all the way to Oklahoma City, if necessary.

"He won't give up," Jim said as he sped to the east side of Anadarko and out to a country road.

"That's my brother-in-law." I laughed, not knowing the half of what I had just said. "Are we getting close?"

"Just one more mile," Jim said calmly, keeping one eye on the road and the other on Brooks in the rearview mirror.

"There it is," Jim exclaimed. He stopped his car, blocking the front end of a one-lane bridge. Martha and I jumped out of Jim's car, ran across the bridge, and opened the door of the immaculately clean Dodge Dart that was parked on the other side. We waved good-bye to Jim and to Brooks and to his cronies as they conceded defeat.

From that one-lane bridge, we bore east on the county road that led us first to Oklahoma City and from there to the land of forever and forever.

EPILOGUE

A half-century has passed since the Phikeia pledge-class lay exhausted in a field somewhere north of Dallas. For the most part, the days have been good. Martha and I are within four years of celebrating a "golden anniversary," having two married daughters and seven lively grandchildren to show for the exchange of our marital vows.

I have learned over the years that finding a lifetime companion is neither science nor art. To some, that initial encounter with a person who eventually becomes one's spouse is nothing more than fate or sheer coincidence, but to those of us who embrace a Christian worldview of life, the events that lead two people to a crossroads where their lives intersect is a manifestation of the ongoing providence of God. I will forever be grateful for the circumstances that brought Martha and me to a place where we could meet, share some defining moments with one another, and become husband and wife. I can't explain how or why it all happened the way it did; I'm simply grateful.

Making career choices is another matter. A person can be far more deliberate in choosing a successful career path than he or she can in selecting an ideal mate. For three years I vacillated between ministry and law, eventually choosing both or neither, depending on how you look at it. While attending law school and for a couple of years after graduation, I was employed as a youth minister for churches in Dallas and Oklahoma City. Overlapping some of those years, I enjoyed a private law practice, operating from an office in our home in Oklahoma City and relying upon Martha to type my legal documents.

But my lifetime professional career ultimately became Christian higher education. For thirty-two years, I was an administrator at Oklahoma Christian College, my *alma mater,* which has now become a Christian liberal arts university. Following President James O. Baird's remarkable tenure, I served twenty-one years as the college's president and chief executive officer, and an additional five years as its chancellor. As you may have already surmised, Martha was an incredible "first lady."

Working at the college proved to be the best of both worlds for me. Drawing upon my legal education, I taught business law, labor law, and constitutional law to our undergraduates, maintaining an active membership with the Oklahoma Bar Association. And yet, I had multiple opportunities every month to preach and minister among churches that had affiliation with Oklahoma Christian.

You may wonder what happened to the college's strict code of student conduct? Well, freshmen no longer have to double-date. That rule changed the year after I graduated. Curfew hours have become more lenient, and sign-out procedures in the residence halls are no longer in force. The old *in loco parentis* policy, where the college stood in the place of the parents, has all but disappeared. There does remain a prohibition on the use of alcoholic beverages, but those who run afoul of the rule are sent to counselors, who try to work with the issue instead of sending the offenders home. Students are treated now as adults, and they are expected to behave as responsible adults.

All undergraduates at Oklahoma Christian continue to attend a daily chapel program as part of their weekly schedule. It is the most prominent bridge between the present and the past, spanning generations of students over six decades. I am hopeful that tradition will never change.

Thirty or more years ago, Martha and I attended a special anniversary for the little church in Shell Knob, Missouri. Isaac and Delia Epperly were both deceased at that time. Since then, the little white-frame church building burned to the ground, and the members have built a new one out on the highway. I hardly knew these people, but I stand deep in their debt.

I don't think about the tragic car/train accident as much as I once did. From my own experiences, it is the classic case that prompts the question, "Why does God allow bad things to happen to good people?" My answer is no more satisfying to me today than it was forty-seven years ago. Job had to struggle with that question centuries ago, and on some level, each of us bumps up against the issue once or more in a lifetime. God understands; I don't.

Epilogue

Awakenings is the third volume in a trilogy of novellas written about events that occurred fifty or more years ago. Although based on true stories and real people, some of the incidents and dialogue have been embellished to weave the storyline into a more readable form. I like to think of the trilogy as historic fiction—tales told by the Missouri boy who grew up playing baseball in the Ozarks. If you enjoyed reading this book, you may wish to explore the two that precede it: *Cardinal Fever* and *Kirby: from the Baseball Field to the Battlefield*. Both are available from the publisher, Tate Publishing, Mustang, Oklahoma, or from your local bookstore.